GW00729905

This compilation copyright © 1999 Lion Publishing

Published by
Lion Publishing plc
Sandy Lane West, Oxford, England
ISBN 0 7459 4037 4

First edition 1999
10 9 8 7 6 5 4 3 2 1 0

A catalogue record for this book is available
from the British Library

Typeset in 12/12.5 Venetian 301
Printed and bound in Singapore

Designer: Philippa Jenkins

secrets of

peace

PEACE MEANS...

...becoming still and silent
...giving love and attention
...knowing yourself
...living for the present
...making wise choices
...practising forgiveness
...reflecting on beauty and truth
...saying a prayer
...seeing the funny side

secrets of

peace

Compiled by
Philip Law

Illustrated by
Grahame Baker Smith

LION
Giftlines

BECOMING STILL
AND SILENT

Turn aside for a while from
your daily employment, escape
for a moment from the tumult
of your thoughts.

Put aside your weighty cares,
let your burdensome distractions
wait, free yourself awhile for
God and rest awhile in him.

ST ANSELM

There is an experience of being
in pure consciousness which gives
lasting peace to the soul. It is an
experience of the Ground or
Depth of being in the Centre of
the soul, an awareness of the
mystery of being beyond sense
and thought, which
gives a sense of
fulfilment, of
finality, of
absolute truth.

BEDE GRIFFITHS

Slow me down, Lord,
Ease the pounding
of my heart by the
quietening of my mind,
Steady my hurried pace
with the vision of the
eternal reach of time.
Give me, amid the
confusion of the day,
the calmness of the
everlasting hills.

ORIN L. CRAIN

Be silent about great things;
let them grow inside you.
Never discuss them: discussion
is so limiting and distracting.
It makes things grow smaller…
Before all greatness be silent —
in art, in music, in religion:
silence.

FRIEDRICH VON HUGEL

In the rush and noise of life,
as you have intervals, step
within yourselves and be still.
Wait upon God and feel his
good presence; this will carry
you through your day's business.

WILLIAM PENN

He who would be serene and pure needs but one thing — detachment.

MEISTER ECKHART

God is the friend of silence.
Trees, flowers, grass grow
in silence.
See the stars, moon and sun,
how they move in silence.

MOTHER TERESA

GIVING LOVE
AND ATTENTION

To love our neighbour is the only
door out of the dungeon of the self.

GEORGE MACDONALD

Freedom from anxiety is characterized by three inner attitudes. If what we have we receive as a gift, and if what we have is to be cared for by God, and if what we have is available to others, then we will possess freedom from anxiety.

RICHARD FOSTER

For it is in giving
that we receive,
it is in loving
that we are loved
and it is in dying
that we are born
to eternal life.

ST FRANCIS

The perfect peace of the holy
angels lies in their love for God
and their love for one another.
This is also the case with all the
saints from the beginning of time.

St Maximus the Confessor

A happiness that is sought for
ourselves alone can never be
found: for a happiness that is
diminished by being shared is
not big enough to make us happy.

Thomas Merton

Happiness is to be found only in the home where God is loved and honoured, where each one loves, and helps, and cares for the others.

THEOPHANES VENARD

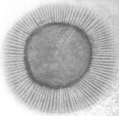

KNOWING YOURSELF

A humble knowledge of yourself
is a surer way to God than an
extensive search after knowledge.

THOMAS A KEMPIS

Do you know why you never stop?
You think, perhaps,
it's a sense of responsibility,
a lack of time to waste,
distaste and scorn for
everything preventing you
from making the best use
of life's brief span.
The simple fact is this:
you are deceiving yourself
and trying to avoid
a self-to-self encounter.

DOM HELDER CAMARA

We can do nothing
if we hate ourselves,
or feel that all our
actions are doomed to
failure because of our
own worthlessness.
We have to take
ourselves, good and
bad alike, on trust
before we can do
anything.

MARTIN ISRAEL

Do not impose on yourself a labour that is beyond your strength, otherwise you will enslave yourself to the need to please others.

JOHN OF APAMEA

If you are humble, nothing will touch you, neither praise nor disgrace, because you know what you are.

MOTHER TERESA

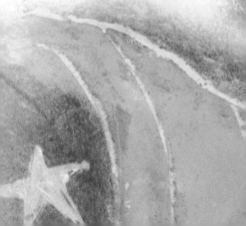

Take yourself as you are, and do not try to live by one part alone and starve the other.

JANET ERSKINE STUART

Living for
the Present

To improve the golden moment
of opportunity, and catch the
good that is within our reach, is
the great art of life.

Samuel Johnson

Accept surprises that upset your
plans, shatter your dreams,
give a completely different turn
to your day and — who knows?
— to your life. It is not chance.
Leave the Father free himself to
weave the pattern of your days.

DOM HELDER CAMARA

He who binds himself to joy
Doth the winged life destroy;
but he who kisses the joy as it flies
Lives in Eternity's sunrise.

WILLIAM BLAKE

Time lost is time
when we have not lived
a full human life,
time unenriched by
experience, creative
endeavour, enjoyment
and suffering.

DIETRICH BONHOEFFER

Do not worry at being worried; but accept worry peacefully. Difficult but not impossible.

JOHN CHAPMAN

Those who face that which is actually before them, unburdened by the past, undistracted by the future, these are they who live, who make the best use of their lives; these are those who have found the secret of contentment.

ALBAN GOODIER

Happy the ones,
and happy they alone,
they, who can call today their own:
They who, secure within, can say,
'Tomorrow do your worst,
for I have lived today.'

JOHN DRYDEN

No man ever sank under the burden of the day. It is when tomorrow's burden is added to the burden of today that the weight is more than a man can bear. Never load yourself so. If you find yourself so loaded, at least remember this: it is your doing, not God's. He begs you to leave the future to him and mind the present.

GEORGE MACDONALD

Anxiety does not empty tomorrow of its sorrows, but only empties today of its strength.

CHARLES HADDON SPURGEON

In every part and corner of our life, to lose oneself is to be gainer; to forget oneself is to be happy.

ROBERT LOUIS STEVENSON

MAKING WISE CHOICES

O Lord, may I be directed what
to do and what to leave undone.

ELIZABETH FRY

I know well the feeling of being
all tense with business and worry.
The only cure is the old one –
'Whenever you have too much
to do, don't do it.'

A.C. Benson

Pruning creates strength, richness, depth, though temporarily pruning hurts and conjures up doubt and fear. It takes a wise gardener to know when and how and how much to cut back a beautiful rose... It takes a wise individual to prune himself or herself according to one's unique needs and timing.

MATTHEW FOX

When one door of happiness closes, another opens; but often we look so long at the closed door that we do not see the one which has been opened for us.

HELEN KELLER

God grant me the serenity
to accept the things I cannot
change, the courage to change
the things I can, and the wisdom
to know the difference.

REINHOLD NIEBUHR
(ADAPTED)

PRACTISING FORGIVENESS

He who cannot forgive others,
breaks the bridge over which
he himself must pass.

CORRIE TEN BOOM

Forgiveness is the key that unlocks the door of resentment and the handcuffs of hate. It is a power that breaks the chains of bitterness and the shackles of selfishness.

CORRIE TEN BOOM

If we will have peace
without a worm in it,
lay we the foundations
of justice and good will.

OLIVER CROMWELL

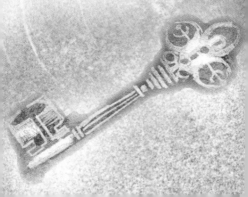

Pardon one another so that later on
you will not remember the injury.
The remembering of an injury is
itself a wrong: it adds to our

anger, feeds our sin and hates
what is good. It is a rusty arrow
and poison for the soul.

St Francis of Paola

REFLECTING ON
BEAUTY AND TRUTH

Peace is always beautiful.

WALT WHITMAN

Love all God's creation, the whole of it and every grain of sand. Love every leaf, every ray of God's light! Love the animals, love the plants, love everything. If you love everything, you will perceive the divine mystery in things. And once you have perceived it, you will begin to comprehend it ceaselessly more and more every day.

FYODOR DOSTOEVSKY

For each truth revealed by
grace, and received with
inward delight and joy, is
a secret murmur of God
in the ear of a pure soul.

WALTER HILTON

The quiet of quiet places is made quieter by natural sounds. In a wood on a still day the quiet is increased by the whisper of the trees.

MARK RUTHERFORD

Creation not only
exists, it also
discharges truth…
Wisdom requires a
surrender, verging
on the mystical,
of a person to the
glory of existence.

GERHARD VON RAD

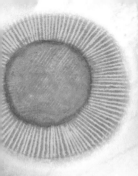

SAYING A PRAYER

Troubles melt away before a
fervent prayer like snow
before the sun.

St John Vianney

If you pray truly, you will
feel within yourself a great
assurance: and the angels
will be your companions.

EVAGRIUS OF PONTUS

The exercise of prayer, in those
who habitually exert it, must
be regarded by us doctors as
the most adequate and normal
of all pacifiers of the mind and
calmers of the nerves.

WILLIAM JAMES

Always long and pray that the
will of God may be fully realized
in your life. You will find that
the man who does this walks in
the land of peace and quietness.

THOMAS A KEMPIS

To thee, O God, we turn for peace... but grant us too the blessed assurance that nothing shall deprive us of that peace, neither ourselves, nor our foolish, earthly desires, nor my wild longings, nor the anxious cravings of my heart.

SØREN KIERKEGAARD

Peace does not mean
the end of all our striving,
Joy does not mean
the drying of our tears;
Peace is the power
that comes to souls arriving
Up to the light where God
Himself appears.

G.A. Studdert Kennedy

Prayer opens up the old wound
which hasn't healed right, eases
in the ointment, and helps it to
heal at last.

TOM WRIGHT

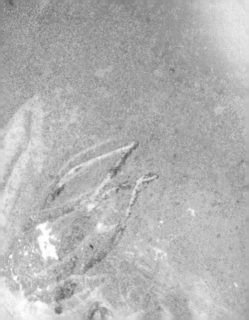

SEEING THE
FUNNY SIDE

It is the heart that is not yet sure
of its God that is afraid to laugh
in his presence.

GEORGE MACDONALD

Laugh and grow strong.

ST IGNATIUS LOYOLA

Laughter is able to mediate
between the infinite magnitude
of our tasks and the limitation
of our strengths.

Jurgen Moltmann

It is a splendid thing to laugh
inwardly at yourself. It is the
best way of regaining your good
humour and of finding God
without further anxiety.

Henri de Tourville